PORT OF LONDON AU

G000230407

NEW BRIDGE
OVER
BENFLEET CREEK

NOTICE IS HEREBY GIVEN

that the new bridge over Benfleet Creek adjacent to the Hard leading from Benfleet to Canvey Island WILL BE OPENED for road traffic on Thursday, 21st May, 1931.

The structure will contain a drawbridge in the centre which will be opened to a width of 60 feet for the passage of vessels. When the drawbridge is closed there will be two navigable openings each 30 feet wide with a headway of 2 feet above High Water of Ordinary Spring Tides for boats and small craft.

Masters of vessels requiring the bridge to be opened during the day shall exhibit a black ball or shape in a position on the vessel where it can best be seen and during the night shall wave a white light horizontally.

On and after 21st May, 1931, the following navigation lights will appear on the bridge :—

WHEN CLOSED.
> Two red lights horizontal in centre of bridge and one white light over the centre of each of the two navigable openings.

WHEN OPEN.
> Two red lights—one on each side of the navigation opening.

By Order,

J. D. RITCHIE

Secretary.

London, E.C. 3.

20th May, 1931.

Best wishes

Norman Bhiman

Bygone Benfleet

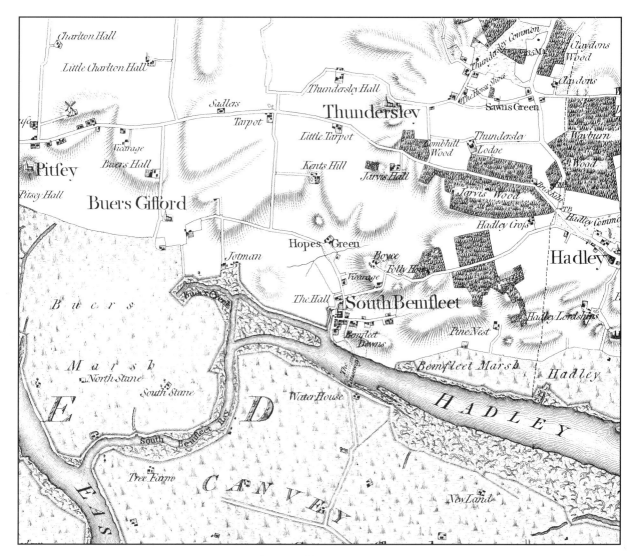

Benfleet and area from the Chapman and André map of 1777.

Bygone
Benfleet

Norman M. Chisman, D.P.A.

Phillimore

1991

Published by
PHILLIMORE & CO. LTD.
Shopwyke Hall, Chichester, Sussex

ISBN 0 85033 779 8

Printed and bound in Great Britain by
BIDDLES LTD.
Guildford, Surrey

To my wife, Vera (Quilter), who lived in, and loved Benfleet all her life.

List of Illustrations

Frontispiece: Benfleet and area from the Chapman and André map of 1777

Preface

When local historian, Dr. Harold Priestley, finished his *History of Benfleet* he gave me every encouragement to produce a modern sequel. As four generations of my wife's family were so involved in the village, she shared his enthusiasm and added her knowledge.

Access to photographs accumulated by the family served as a basis, supplemented by the collection taken in 1925 by Henry Clubb, a local photographer, and much work and slide photography undertaken in the 1970s and 1980s by the late John Brooks, a member of the Benfleet and District Historical Society.

Two local postcard enthusiasts gave great assistance: Ron Mead, one of the leading dealers in the country, together with Bill Hurrell, a Society member, and many of their cards are included.

Iris (Knightley) Sugg, her husband Eddie and sister Doris, provided not only photographs but local knowledge and identification, particularly welcome with the sudden and untimely death of my wife, Vera, in September 1990.

Other photographs and assistance came from Kath Fisher, Bobby Fisher and Jack Phillips, Doug and Dorothy Wilson, Nita Land, Jackie Barnes, John Downer, Fred Cutler, and many more, particularly members of the Society.

Vic Harrison, Ted Purdy and Harry Russell helped with sketches and the proprietors of the *Anchor* have been helpful. I befriended the Benfleet Camera Club, and Ray Davis and David Berry contributed, as did Chas Rawlings.

Edward Clack, of Airborne Camera, readily agreed to the use of one of his current aerial photographs, by courtesy of the Essex Wildlife Trust. Essex Record Office supplied the photograph of Anchor Meadows Fair and the Planning Department of Essex County Council prepared the sketch of the *Anchor* structure. The picture depicting the opening of Benfleet Downs is reproduced by courtesy of the *Evening Echo*.

The research seems to have brought many friends and relations closer. Apart from the assistance of my immediate family, I have now met and been helped by members on the Land side.

Whilst portraying bygone Benfleet and analysing some of its development, I hope I have been able to record, and readers will be able to sense, an unhurried, colourful, caring and proud community of the kind which, nationally, is fast disappearing under an avalanche of cars, monotonous housing and a rush to go ... where?

Introduction

Benfleet, the name

The name originated about one thousand five hundred years ago when Saxons first arrived and settled in the area. Their small craft entered the Thames, where they found a creek between Canvey Island and the mainland. Here were marshes with plenty of wildfowl for food and a good supply of reeds for roof thatching. Inland, two thickly-wooded valleys provided timber for both huts and boats, while streams ensured an adequate water supply. The name *Beamfleote* arose as the site was a creek with adjoining woods: *beam* in Anglo-Saxon means a tree, and *fleote* a stretch of water. In the course of time the spelling varied and documents show Beamflet, Bemflet, Benfleota and Bienflet. Bemfleet was used on maps by John Norden (1548-1625) and by Chapman and André in their Essex Atlas of 1777. Variations occurred until 1855 when the new railway used Benfleet for its station and timetable.

In early days a small and separate community coming mostly from Benfleet set itself up four miles to the north. This was called Little, and later North, Benfleet so the original village was known as South Benfleet. North Benfleet is now a rural area, not covered by this book.

Roman Times

After Julius Caesar came to Britain in 55 B.C. the Romans constructed a road from London to Colchester. A secondary highway, from this road, connected the Roman military station at Chelmsford with Canvey Island, through Rettendon and Runwell, over the rise at North Benfleet, crossing the present A13 near Sadlers Farm roundabout. In 1971 the A130 was constructed along this route from Sadlers Farm roundabout, crossing Jotmans Lane, the railway and the creek to Canvey. During this work a member of the Benfleet Historical Society found, on the Benfleet side of the creek, pottery, roof tiles, a bronze pin, bone and unopened shellfish. Experts identified first and second century (late Roman) pottery and some Saxon and medieval pottery as late as the 13th and 14th centuries. Not only had Romans settled here, but apparently they had constructed their creek viaduct on the same route as that selected by planners in 1971.

The following sketches show: The site of the Roman finds, the line of the Roman road.

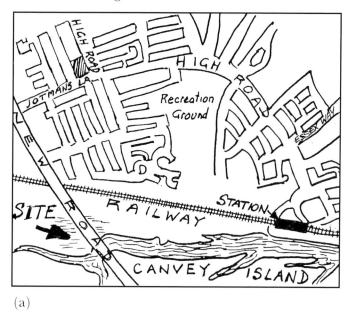

(a)

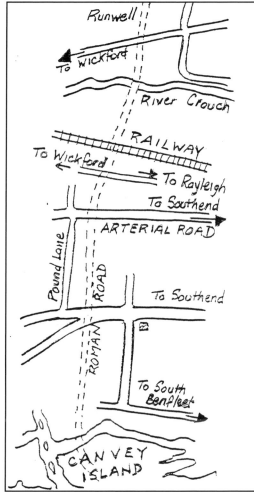

(a) The site of the Roman finds.

(b) The line of the Roman road.

(b)

Battle of Benfleet

An important battle took place in Benfleet in 893. A stronghold had been established by the Danes some years before, to which remnants of their Great Army returned after defeats by King Alfred's son, Edward, at Farnham in Kent and at Iver, Buckinghamshire. The Benfleet stronghold (see sketch below) was still a threat to London, despite reduced numbers, so in 893 Edward and his brother-in-law brought a force from the capital which stormed and took the fortress. They burnt the Danish boats in Benfleet creek, and the charred remains of these, together with skeletons, were discovered in 1855 when navvies were driving piles for the railway track.

Some seventy years after the battle, Ethelweard, great-grandson of Alfred's elder brother Ethelred, wrote this account in the Anglo-Saxon Chronicle:

> The fortress at Beamfleote had ere this been constructed by Haestan and he was at the same time gone out to plunder and the Great Army was therein. Then they [the English] came thereto and put the Army to flight and stormed the fortress and took all that was within it as well as the women and children also, and brought the whole to London and all the ships they either broke in pieces or burned or brought to London and Rochester, and they brought the wife of Haestan and his two sons to the King ...

Dr. Harold Priestley in his *History of Benfleet* details evidence to establish the identification of the site of the stronghold as follows:

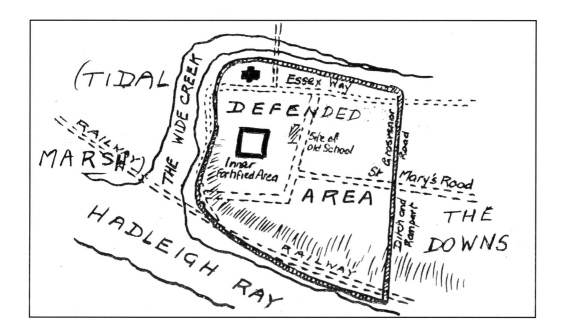

The following conjectural sketch of the camp appeared in the third journal of the Benfleet Historical Society.

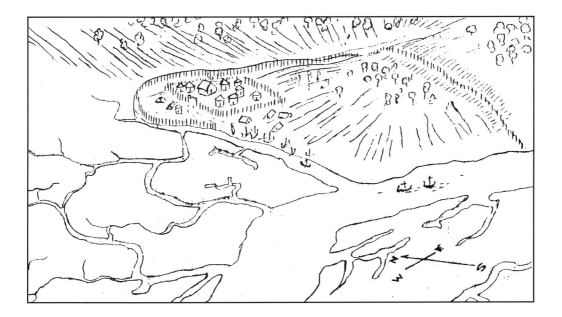

Benfleet church and Westminster

Barking Abbey was founded in 666 by Erkenwald, Bishop of London. It prospered until 870 when the Danes, who sought to remove all traces of the Christian faith, attacked and put the nuns to death. In 878 Barking passed into Danish hands as a result of a treaty between Alfred and the Danish chief Guthrum. After the Battle of Benfleet, Edward drove the Danes from Essex, and Barking Abbey, rebuilt in 930, was granted Benfleet.

Churches were often built on the site of battles and it is probable that this happened at Benfleet. This first church would have been a small rectangular building, and its subsequent development is shown in the sketch below. Sir Charles Nicholson, honorary architect to Benfleet parish, referred in 1924, in the parish magazine, to old foundations said to exist in the churchyard to the south-east of the present chancel. The nuns of Barking Abbey would probably have installed a priest here but names of vicars are recorded only from 1189.

In 1066 King William was crowned. The following year he confirmed the retention by Barking Abbey of most of its lands, but granted Benfleet to Westminster Abbey, who retained it until Henry VIII dissolved the monasteries in 1536. The property of Westminster, including South Benfleet manor, was taken over by the Crown and in 1540, the year Barking Abbey was destroyed, the manor was re-granted to the dean and chapter of Westminster. Although Westminster sold the manor in 1799 to the Rev. John Mayor, they have retained the advowson of the church (the right to appoint the vicar) until this day.

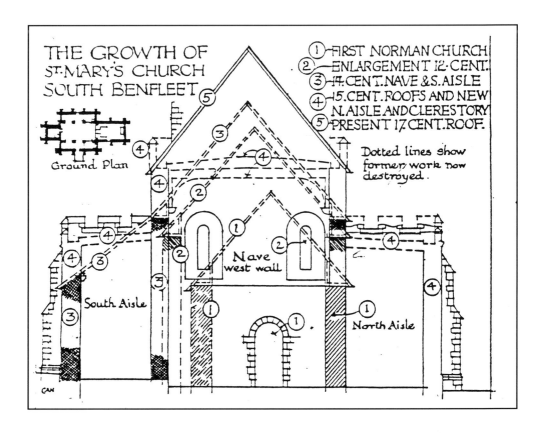

THE GROWTH OF ST. MARY'S CHURCH SOUTH BENFLEET

1. FIRST NORMAN CHURCH
2. ENLARGEMENT 12. CENT.
3. 14. CENT. NAVE & S. AISLE
4. 15. CENT. ROOFS AND NEW N. AISLE AND CLERESTORY
5. PRESENT 17. CENT. ROOF.

Ground Plan

Dotted lines show former work now destroyed.

Nave west wall

South Aisle

North Aisle

Early Life in the Manors of Benfleet

In 1086 the Domesday Book shows that there were two manors in Benfleet. Sweyne (later Jarvis Hill) was the smaller, lying roughly between Kents Hill Road and Thundersley Park Road, which explains the unsymmetrical road pattern of the area.

The other, encompassing the rest of Benfleet, was the manor of Hall Farm, owned by the abbot of Westminster. The manor house, The Hall, which is shown on early maps, was on the present site of the Methodist church and St Mary's Service Station. The bailiff, who managed the farm, lived at The Hall and had his own footbridge across the brook to St Mary's church with his private door in the north wall, now bricked up but still visible. The farm had a large barn fronting High Road which, with a thatched roof, eventually replaced by corrugated iron, can still be remembered by villagers. It stood there for about four hundred years. The farm itself was quite extensive, including the present Hall Farm Road and Brook Road, taking in the Recreation Ground and some of the housing estates as far west as Jotmans. Apart from the farm, the rest of the manor of Hall Farm included most of South Benfleet between Tarpots and Victoria House corner, down to the Thames. Within the manor there would be other farms held by men, as tenants, from the prior, the lord of the manor. A tenant was allowed to pass the land on to his heir – who could inherit if he paid the lord an entry fine, one of a multitude of feudal dues. Tenants had to spend three days every week tending the lord's demesne – Hall Farm – where at Easter they had to attend the manor court. In Domesday Book the entry for Hall Farm showed that in 1086 the abbot had two ploughs (16 oxen) and the men of the village held five ploughs (60 oxen). There were 15 villeins (villagers with about thirty acres) and 12 bordars (cottagers with some four to eight acres).

In this sketch, taken from Harold Priestley's *History of Benfleet*, Hall Farm, the church, and the *Anchor* are dominant. High Street was then Church Street and petered out at the creek. Much of the village was along East Street (Essex Way) and the path to Canvey is shown.

Trading

Benfleet creek gave ready access to the extensive forests nearby, and much timber was extracted, primarily for shipbuilding. Logs from Shipwright's Woods were loaded onto sailing boats at the wharf adjoining the *Hoy and Helmet* ('hoy' meaning sailboat, and 'helmet' a quay) and taken to Leigh and other boat-building villages. Much timber went to Westminster Abbey. Records there show how busy Benfleet was in 1559 and give an interesting breakdown of costs:

Felling, cutting and binding 200 loads	£33
Carriage to waterside (Church creek)	£10
Wharfage (use of wharf)	£20
Carriage by water to Westminster	£ 6

Early settlers lived by the sea and many cottagers at Benfleet creek were fishermen as well as hoymen. Oysters were also produced in the creek. The inlet of water to Hopes Green (at the present junior school) also resulted in the establishment there in the 16th century of the first cottages for fishermen. Evidence of this early trading was highlighted when excavating for the extension of the present wine shop at the War Memorial. Three finds were made: broken clay smoking pipes which had been discarded; quantities of broken shell from eating oysters; and several feet of sawdust, proving the existence of a sawpit. The logs from Shipwright's Woods would have been cut here, and taken down the hill to the waiting hoys in the creek.

Smuggling was part of the livelihood of this area for centuries, particularly when agriculture was in decline. In 1733 Mr. Vaughan, lord of the manor of Jarvis Hall, claimed as wreck some casks of spirits found sunk at Benfleet creek. Customs stated that they made the discovery in a rill leading to the creek and that the casks were contraband as they were secured to stakes. They 'saw at a distance a boat with five men in her,-two of whom are believed to have been Layzell and Gardner, notorious smugglers'. The rill probably adjoined the *Hoy and Helmet*, which was often linked with smugglers. There was also reputed to be a tunnel to the adjoining church.

The Customs Service was set up initially on a local basis, becoming a national service in 1671. The main office was at Colchester, with branches at Maldon, Burnham and a sub-office at Leigh. The *Crown*, adjoining the *Hoy and Helmet*, only became a pub in the 18th century and is believed to have been a customs house before this, eminently sited in what was, in the 16th and 17th centuries, the busiest port in Essex.

During the 19th and well into the 20th century, hay from Canvey Island was ferried by majestic Thames barges from Benfleet creek to London for the cab-horses, and their manure was brought back for the farms.

Population and Development

Until the 18th century Benfleet remained rural and sparsely populated. The estimated figure for 1600 was 281 and for 1700 280. In 1801 there were still only 338 inhabitants; by 1851 this had risen to 570 and in 1901 the total was 1,024. By 1921 the number was 1,918, in 1931 it was 4,170 and in 1991 the figure for South Benfleet has been estimated as 15,000, and 84,900 for Castle Point.

After World War One, housing estates started to develop and the gap between the village, the church and Hopes Green rapidly disappeared. Frank Barnes sold land to Inverson and Morgan who built the Seaview estate consisting of St Mary's Road, Highcliffe Road and Mill Hill in 1927-9. At Hopes Green in 1928, where other estates were developing, Messrs. Raffin and Bonsor built The Parade, shops in High Road between Richmond Avenue and Kents Hill Road. Later, in 1936, C. S. Wiggins built Jotmans Estate at Cemetery Corner.

Local Government

In the 16th century local government began to pass from the manor to the church and churchwardens, assisted by a group of parishioners who met in the vestry and became known as the Vestry Committee. The first book of the South Benfleet Vestry Minutes begins at Easter 1679 and in it are listed the names of those appointed churchwardens, overseer of the poor, constable and surveyor. Ordinary villagers were elected annually to these voluntary posts. Minutes recording resignations and reluctance show some 'arm twisting' was necessary to fill them. Constables were often drawn from the tradesmen of the village. A good example of other officers was James Matthews, hoyman, who lived in the parish for 44 years. He was Overseer of the Poor from 1708 to 1713 and again from 1718 to 1719. Surveyor of Highways in 1721 and 1723, and in 1728 was churchwarden.

His epitaph in the churchyard reads:

> Sixty three years our Hoyman sail'd merrily around;
> Fourty-four liv'd Parishioner where he's Aground;
> Five Wife's bear him thirty-three Children. Enough
> Land another as honest before he gets off.

Around the middle of the 19th century the responsibilities of the Vestry started to diminish. In 1894 the election of the first South Benfleet Parish Council took place, and individuals on it made great contributions to the development of the area. The rapid expansion of the area caused by the post-war building boom called for a more organised system of local government to be implemented; thus in 1929 the Benfleet Urban District Council was created from a merger of Benfleet and neighbouring villages, Hadleigh and Thundersley. The Council survived until 1974 when it joined with the administration of Canvey Island to produce Castle Point District Council.

Community Life

From the 16th century a fair was held annually on a Saturday in late August. In 1665 it was cancelled, by Sir Henry Appleton, lord of the manor, because of the plague. Thus Benfleet remained immune from the disease, although it was prevalent in Hornchurch and Colchester. The fair became the village fête and in the 20th century was held on the *Anchor* meadows. It was often preceded by a procession similar to the present carnival. Gypsies brought a travelling fair at Whitsun to land adjoining The Hall, near the site of the present Methodist Church. There was a large elm tree on the site and gypsies would collect beneath it in the evenings, singing songs accompanied by accordions and violins. Early community life centred round the three pubs, the *Anchor*, built in 1380, the 15th-century *Hoy and Helmet* and the *Crown* (18th century). In 1892 the villagers, acting together as shareholders in a public company, acquired a building adjoining the church. They named it the Village Institute and used it as a public hall for concerts, parties, Brownies, Sunday School and church hall for 40 years. It was demolished in 1932.

At the corner of Brook Road and High Road there was a cinema. Later, part at the rear became the Barn Club with billiard tables. Next door, further down Brook Road, Benfleet Hall was built in 1922. This was the venue for entertainment, old people's dinners and dances. In 1936 it was the Bay Country Club, and Benfleet Tennis Club used the two courts at the rear. During the war it became a clothing factory, for which it is still used today.

Roads

The early road pattern was of paths from Pitsea (thence London) along Jotmans Lane, passing Hopes Green to the War Memorial, formerly The Cross. As the present A13 developed the main route to the west used the link road from Cemetery Corner to Tarpots. This road was first called North Street (from The Cross), then London Road and finally, in 1932, High Road, from Tarpots to the War Memorial.

The only early access from the village to Hadleigh and Southend was up Vicarage Hill, even steeper then than it is today. The road from The Cross towards Hadleigh was called East Street, then the Endway (as it ended in fields). In 1937 this road was rebuilt and extended to give access to Hadleigh, and was renamed Essex Way. From The Cross the original road to Canvey turned up Essex Way, then right along School Lane (Clib Lane until the school was built in 1845) and then over the Downs to the causeway or ferry.

The road from The Cross, down the hill, was originally Church Street and is now High Street. Earlier this only went as far as the *Hoy and Helmet* where it ended with the timber wharf and hardway for launching boats. The present narrow passage opposite the church side entrance, The Close, was in fact the main road for that part of the village. The extension of High Street from the *Hoy and Helmet* towards the station, and now known as Lower High Street, resulted from the coming of the railway. The road over the Downs was legally diverted in 1830, when the the railway company was acquiring land for its line.

The High Road between the church and the *Anchor* was raised in 1926 to prevent flooding. In 1932 Knightley's shop and the Village Institute at the entrance to the church were demolished and the road down the hill was widened. Further widening took place in 1966 when shops adjoining the churchyard were demolished. An unplanned 'improvement' took place in 1969 when a lorry hit and removed part of the *Crown* which was reopened at the end of that year, becoming the *Half-Crown* after a renaming competition among patrons.

Early traffic for Canvey was delayed by having to cross the causeway when the tide was out. When cars got stuck in the mud ferrymen could charge well for rescuing them with horses.

The first bridge opened on 21 May 1931, but traffic was still forced to queue: boats had precedence over road traffic, so the bridge frequently had to be opened, and the railway level crossing gates also caused delays. On 5 February 1962 an underpass under the station ended the level crossing problem and the last traffic delay from the swing bridge was in November 1968, although the new permanent bridge did not open until 1973.

The Canvey Road from Sadlers Farm roundabout was opened in April 1973, and this gave Benfleet High Road a respite from traffic congestion which, however, soon returned.

Public Road Transport

Public transport by horse and carriage was provided in the 1880s by George Land, proprietor of the *Anchor*. He kept four horses which were all needed on the steep and winding Vicarage Hill to Hadleigh. This service continued from the *Anchor* until the coming of motor coach services.

In the 1920s Pearce's coaches appeared, as did the Thundersley, Hadleigh and District buses. These were taken over in 1932 by the Bridge family to become the green buses of Benfleet and District Motor Services which alternated every 15 minutes with the red buses of Westcliff Motor Services. In 1952 the Eastern National Omnibus Company took over the red and green buses, as well as Canvey and District Motor Transport Company and City Coach Company. In 1955 Eastern National and Southend Corporation Transport agreed to pool services and receipts,and this continued until terminated under the Transport Act of 1986. On 29 July 1990 Thamesway Ltd. took over the operation of most of the Eastern National routes in the area.

The Railway

One of the major reasons for the development of Benfleet was the coming of the railway. In 1854 the line from London first went as far as Tilbury for the docks and the pleasure gardens at Rosherville near Gravesend. The extension to Pitsea, Benfleet and Leigh opened on 1 July 1855. For 30 years passengers to London had to travel via Tilbury as the marsh areas of Bulphan Fen, Horndon, made engineering difficult, and shareholders were reluctant to invest. On 1 June 1888 the direct line between Benfleet and Fenchurch Street eventually opened.

The first station at Benfleet was wooden and was built adjoining the ferry terminus to Canvey. This was burnt down in 1903 by sparks from the steam engines and was rebuilt in its present position in 1912. Electrification started in November 1961 and came into full service in June 1962.

Street Lighting

The advent of gas saw the issue of providing public street lighting raised at the Parish Council year after year. Finally, in 1926, it was agreed that 32 lamps would be provided at a cost of £292 17s. 6d.

The Fire Brigade

A voluntary force started in 1924 with a hand cart stored at the *Anchor* stables. The Captain was W. H. Shepherd and the crew included Bill and Bert Blake, and Ted and George Land. When they collected enough to buy an engine in 1925 this was also stationed at the *Anchor*. When a resident of South View Road donated his garage to house the new acquisition the whole village turned out to cheer the eight volunteers who stood inside the building and carried it along the High Road to the land next to the *Anchor*.

Fire calls were made to the *Anchor* when a maroon was set off to call the crew and everyone rushed to watch the brave volunteers in their fine brass helmets, stop-watches in hand to check their call-out time. Ted would be driving and George ringing the bell.

In 1928 the Parish Council agreed a penny rate towards the cost of a fire station and in 1931 one was built at Hadleigh. Ted Land and Harold Layzell were the first full-time members to be appointed and Ted stayed at Hadleigh until he retired in 1964.

Post Offices

The first post office was at Simon Daines's cottage, later the site of the Institute Hall, near the main entrance to the church.

In the mid-1800s the post office was in the brick-built shop opposite the present station. The postmaster was Sid Lawrence, who had two daughters, Jane and Mabel. In 1913, after Charlie Brand stopped using part of the *Anchor* as a shop, Laura Brand (née Land) let the premises to the Lawrences as a post office. When Sid died his two daughters carried on the business taking an active part in village life. Jane was the post mistress, assisted by Mabel, when she retired as a headmistress, and they lived in adjoining rooms of the *Anchor*. She had a lending library and for tuppence a week villagers borrowed a book and were trusted to bring it back on time.

The sorting office was at the rear, in what was formerly the stables and if Reg Pudney, the postman, was busy, people went up the yard to collect their own letters. In 1950 the post office was taken over by Mr. Pratt and eventually it moved to the present shop in High Road, opposite St Mary's Close.

At Hopes Green the original post office was in the premises now occupied by Belgravia Florist, which explains the position of the telephone kiosk. The post office moved to its present location after the parade of shops was built in 1928.

Education

In 1810 there were 30 children being educated in dame schools in Benfleet. The National School was established in Clib Lane (School Lane) in 1845 when the vicar, the Rev. John Phelps, succeeded in raising £420, and Westminster Abbey paid for the school equipment. The two school buildings were to the south of the lane, where there is now a large public car park. One of the best-known headmasters (from 1893 to 1923) was Robert Hall. When he retired he ran a private school in Avondale Road, while his daughter Gladys had a kindergarten in the same house.

The National School officially closed in 1927, when the present school, South Benfleet County Junior School, was built in High Road. However the two old buildings continued to be used for some lessons, and for evening classes, church and parish meetings. Opposite the buildings, St Mary's church erected a new hall, which has now been replaced by houses.

Between the wars there were two private schools in Benfleet. One, run by Miss Steggles, was up a small lane opposite St Mary's Service Station and was called Stanley House. This transferred to Vicarage Hill but the name Stanley House went with it. The other was up the west side of Station Road, and was run by Miss Howard. The building remains today.

The junior school continues today, the only addition to the area being the building of Jotmans Hall County Primary School in 1973, in High Road north of Cemetery Corner.

Benfleet Downs

One of the last acts of the Benfleet Parish Council on 6 June 1929, was to purchase 30 acres of the downs. The owner, Frank Barnes, readily concurred as his family, living in Suttons Farm, had already allowed public access to the area. On 14 July 1934 the official opening took place, and in the programme Walter Bingham wrote:

> To have lost to posterity this beautiful space would have been a tragedy indeed and its closing by building or otherwise would have been to extinguish the eyes of Benfleet. A pious hope has often been expressed that at some time in the future, the authorities concerned may get possession of the whole of the slopes from Benfleet to Leigh and thus preserve for ever to the people a vista unrivalled anywhere in Europe and perpetuating for all time to these northern shores of the Thames a marine history which commenced with the British Coracle, continuing with Phoenician and Roman Galley, Norse Dragon, Galleon, Clipper, Benfleet Hoy and the most up-to-date battleship and liner, which have, since the beginning of civilization passed in review before these Downs.

How happy he would be to know that far-sighted local authorities have turned that pious hope into reality. On 18 May 1987 Hadleigh Castle Country Park was opened with 458 acres stretching from Benfleet Downs to Leigh-on-Sea station, and much more designated for acquisition.

The *Anchor*

The original name of the pub was the *Blue Anchor*, shown in Quarter Sessions records of 1770. The *Anchor* has been the centre of much village activity, particularly from 1875 when George Land took over, until 1964, when the family left. During that time the family included the Tuffields, who ran the village shop from 1879 to 1934, the Rev. L. Houghton, vicar 1942-50, and the Brands and Quilters (the author's wife's family). For a century the well at the *Anchor* was the main water supply, until negotiations in 1899 by the Parish Council persuaded the railway company to make their resources available to the public. The *Anchor* was also the first building in Benfleet to be lit by gas.

During 1989 the new proprietor, Geoff Frith, renovated the building. Exposed first-floor joists, which may now be seen from the bar, enabled the Essex County Council Historic Building Section to date the jointing as *c*.1380. Uncovered original plaster of the internal walls revealed a child's fingerprints which could be up to 600 years old. Upstairs an original coat of arms on the wall beams was uncovered, as were medieval windows. Breaking through the second-floor ceiling revealed a magnificent 14th-century crownpost roof of four major and two secondary bays in substantial oak timber with 17th-century painting on the underside of the tie beams.

The medieval windows were facing the stables, which suggests this would have been the front of the building, not the back as now. This view is supported by the discovery, in 1973, of a handless and footless skeleton of a criminal, when a service trench was being dug in the road between the *Anchor* and the War Memorial. He would have been buried to the rear, not the (present) front of the building. With this evidence it might be assumed that the road from Cemetery Corner went between the *Anchor* and the stables before going along School Lane to Canvey. Alternatively there may have been a central courtyard, instead of the present backyard, with access from High Road or via the former covered way passage for vehicles through the *Anchor* from the War Memorial.

The sketch by the Historic Buildings Section of the original structure of the *Anchor* shows another section, since demolished, which would have extended into the present High Road towards the church. This was either burnt down in a fire or removed for road improvement. The close proximity of this building to the church suggests that it was used for religious or public purposes which explains the high standard of workmanship, as Westminster Abbey would have London workmen with the required skills. It may have housed early pilgrims from East Anglia, who are known to have crossed to Canterbury at this point.

The Peasants' Revolt of 1381 was triggered by the imposition of the Poll Tax. The rebellion started in Fobbing , and eventually converged on London where the Chancellor of the Exchequer was hanged. When it was over, Thomas Spragge of South Benfleet 'and others of the same place' were tried before Judge Tresilian at Chelmsford.

Local justice was administered from the Manor Court which probably took place at the Manor Hall. Priestley writes:

> During the revolt many manor halls were burnt down and manor rolls, which the peasants thought were the evidences of their servitude, were burnt with them. The Manor Hall in South Benfleet ... was probably near the site of the present Methodist Church. It is doubtful what happened to the Hall and to the rolls that must have been housed there, since the earliest manor rolls of South Benfleet that survive are those of 1407. It may be that the peasants destroyed both hall and rolls on their progress from Shoebury to London.

The finds at the *Anchor* had not been made when Dr. Priestley was writing; it is now known, however, that *c*.1380 the present *Anchor* was built, of considerable size and high-class workmanship. Recent entry to the roof timbers and crown posts reveal no blackening with residential smoke, this suggesting long-term public use. It is probable that Harold Priestley was right: thus the Manor House/Court House of Hall Farm was destroyed in

1381 and the *Anchor* was then built to function, among other church or public purposes, as the Manor Court. The bailiff would have occupied, at the farm, a building which replaced the Manor House and this became The Hall, or Benfleet Hall, shown on maps of the 19th and 20th centuries.

A walk round Benfleet

The photographs that follow are in ordered sequence, to form a pictorial walk through Benfleet.

The start is at the ferry, between Canvey Island and Benfleet, the scene of much activity, with access by boat or stepping stones.

The building of the bridges is shown, as are the changes as one walks up Ferry Road to the level crossing. The railway, including the stations, is illustrated.

This is followed by the lower High Street and Church creek, where houseboats and little shops may be seen.

Reaching the bottom of the hill of High Street, two of the local pubs are examined: the *Hoy and Helmet* and the *Crown*. Details of old shops and their demolition are also shown.

At the top of the hill, the War Memorial, and the crossroads at the focal point of the village are portrayed. Many activities centred round the *Anchor* are illustrated, indicating its leading rôle in the community. Heading north from the War Memorial the many old buildings of East Street (Essex Way) are shown.

Returning to the crossroads, there is a section about the church before covering High Road and Vicarage Hill. The route continues along High Road, to Cemetery Corner, and then as far as Tarpots Corner.

This is followed by pictures of some roads, such as Thundersley Park, Hope and Hall Farm.

The final section deals with group pictures of the clubs, organisations and school classes that gave backbone to much of the village structure. It finishes with a miscellany of interesting items such as First World War bombs, old newspaper extracts and aerial views.

1. Buses on the Canvey Island side of the ferry in 1925. Alighting passengers then faced either the stepping stones, or the boat, depending on the state of the tide.

2. F. W. B. Hester, who developed the Winter Gardens on Canvey, built a monorail across the island in the position of the present Central Wall Road. It was horse-driven but later electrified, and went into liquidation in 1906. This was one of the coaches being brought across the ferry in 1903.

3. People of all stations had to risk the stepping stones at low tide. Some of the original stones have been placed in concrete at the side of the present Council Offices at Canvey. This photograph dates from 1911.

4. The site of the ferry in 1991.

5. Ferryman Fred Edwards rows over his passengers in 1925, charging 1d., and 2d. for bicycles. There were two rowing boats and two punts. The ferry was originally owned by Mr. Knight, then Jack Polley, then by Mr. Theobald from Canvey, and Kiff Lazell. Another ferryman was Jess Cripps.

6.   In 1929 the creek froze. As we can see, the journey was somewhat perilous and would have difficulty in passing the present Department of Transport regulations!

7. The queue at Whitsun, 1926. Steam trains, on day excursions, brought large crowds particularly from the east end of London. It was not unusual to have to wait an hour for the ferry crossing.

8. Three boats are busy in 1925 but there is still a long queue on the Canvey side and more people are streaming down the pedestrian path which still exists today. These lovely barges usually moored about this spot.

9. One of the Thames barges in Benfleet creek being loaded with hay from Canvey, bound for London.   A boy would be
perched on the stack to guide the helmsman at the back. This photograph was taken in   1925.

10.   This very early picture shows a barge ready to leave while the mother cow shows concern for her straying youngster.

11. One of the highlights of the year was the annual regatta in the creek with boating and swimming races. This is the regatta in 1909.

12. Benfleet Yacht Club was founded in 1922. Its headquarters was this converted Thames sailing barge, or sprittee, named *Soar* and seen here in 1925. Later a schooner named *Hygeia*, a Port Health Authority boat from Gravesend, was used.

13. Benfleet Yacht Club headquarters in 1945 was this ex-Trinity House Lightvessel No. 35 which was moored just by the station. This had to be moved when the underpass at the station was put in and when the non-opening bridge was built. In 1984 a permanent building was erected on Canvey saltings and this ship is now in the Medway near Rochester bridge.

14. These two public buses, seen here in Ferry Road, 1925, between the ferry and the station, were known understandably as the boneshakers. The thatched buildings on the left were part of Leigh Building Supply wharf.

15. The reconstruction of Ferry Road in 1930 – this provided the access road to the first bridge over the creek.

16. The first bridge being built in 1930. This scheme cost £15,000. It was known as Calvin Bridge after Brigadier General Calvin, the Lord Lieutenant of Essex, who performed the pile-driving ceremony in May 1930. In this view a car has got stuck in the mud, as often happened, and the tide is coming in. It will rise another three feet, as can be seen from the algae on the bridge support posts.

17.   The Chairman of the Essex County Council, Alderman J. H. Burrows, J.P., opens the bridge on 21 May 1931.

18.   The author was among the crowd on opening day and recalls the excitement, particularly as all children had the day off school.

19. A sailing barge edges through Calvin bridge on the first day of operation.

20. When the bridge was built, Fred Edwards was made redundant as a ferryman, but was given a part to play on the opening day and was then employed by the council to lower the barriers and open the bridge. This operation took three minutes.

21. The return fare to Southend in 1937 was 6d. The house at the top is Brecon House in St Mary's Road, and still exists. It was built in 1926 by the Barnes family who owned the Downs. Brecon House was a replica of a farmhouse at which they had once stayed and was built with concrete and flint, but no bricks.

22. This 1924 picture shows the 'between tide' problem. People are waiting either for the tide to ebb or for enough water for the boats. The condition of the adjoining road added to the perils of the crossing for vehicles and horses.

23. In May 1972 the second bridge was under construction. The old bridge ceased opening for boats in 1968, and the new bridge came into use in 1973.

24. The old wooden railway station, down by the ferry, before it was burnt down on 3 March 1903. Note the two spritties with sails furled. The goods train is operating on the sidings and the passenger line is between the two buildings.

25. The down (Southend) platform of the pre-1903 station.

26. The down platform in the previous
picture still remains in 1991. The station
buildings can be seen on the left.

27.   The signal box which was at the London end of the old station, photographed in 1905.

28.   This was the scene in 1909. A new station was built on the embankment to the left in 1912. The old signal box is visible. Station Terrace, top left, remains the same in 1991.

HE CREEK, SOUTH BENFLEET.

29.   The new station in the year it opened, 1912. The signal box has been moved to become part of the station.

30. Pedestrians stroll through the level crossing in 1930. When the gates closed the footbridge had to be used, so many tried to squeeze through at the last minute. The children on the bridge are seen in a favourite pastime – waiting for the train to stop and engulf them in a cloud of smoke and steam.

31. These cars, an Austin Seven and a Singer, are waiting to go over to Canvey in 1930.

32. A steam train leaves Benfleet station for Southend in 1930.

33. In the coal sidings at Benfleet, Jack Polley (left) and Fred Edwards (centre) show with pride their replacement for the horses.

34. In 1920 cabbies waited outside the station for passengers. Cliff Hart is at the back. In front is Bill Nunn, from a well-known Benfleet family.

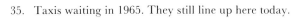

35. Taxis waiting in 1965. They still line up here today.

36. Up Station Road the cart waits outside the slaughterhouse on the right. The two buildings on the left are there today, the higher one originally being Miss Howard's school.

37. Station Terrace in 1919.

38.   Staff pose for their photograph in 1912 among all the meat which traditionally hung outside the butcher's shop.

39.   Looking down Station Road in 1958 as a steam train arrives. The water in the background is known as Amazon creek.

40. Station Road today shows much change from the previous picture.

41. A view from Station Terrace in 1919 shows the signal box, station and station buildings.

42. Staff outside their new station in 1912. Powell's restaurant is on the left and Cash Drapery Stores on the right. In the centre is the grain store later used as an auction room.

43. The same view in 1990 shows how many buildings remain.

44.   In 1925 the booking office only had one entrance, in the centre-left. The porch to the right was the front door to the station-master's house.

45.   O. I. C. Powell had this restaurant, seen here in 1925, and another at Winter Gardens, Canvey, as well as a refreshment hut on the Canvey end of the bridge approach road. The family catered for parties and weddings, making everything in their kitchen – even their own ice cream.

46. This photograph of 1925 shows the Cash Drapery Stores, which around 1930 became Shiner and Holmes' shop with a photographic studio.

47. Today the building, with glass sides, is a car showroom.

48.   These two men are waiting to go into Marie Welsh's little barber's shop (1925). When she moved nearer the *Crown* Lucy Chappell used this office to take orders for coal. The hut next door was occupied by Mr. Bishop, a clock repairer, and the one beyond was built by Tommy Ross for 'Shoey' Sheppard, the cobbler.

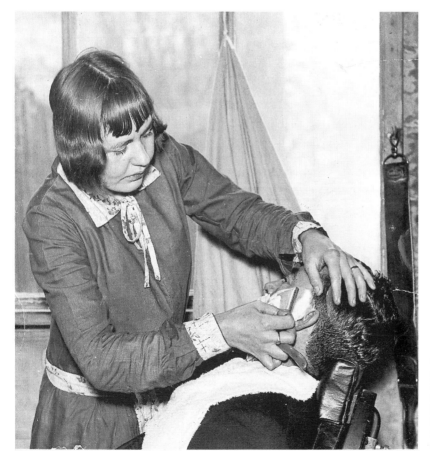

49.   Marie Welsh, at the age of 16, took over her father's hairdressing business when he died. She was one of Benfleet's characters – a match for all her customers – and no-one tried any nonsense with Marie. She married Bill Nunn, horse cab driver.

50.   Looking from the station in 1925, W. T. Lamb (and before that T. E. Ross) used the wharf for timber and building materials. In the background, left, are the two school buildings.

51.   The same view, in 1990.

52. The white building on the left is Wharf Cottage, said to have been built on two barges. The black cottage was home for Nurse Revell and Queenie Killingback. Next was Maurice Upson, estate agent, and the last hut on the right was used by Charlie Idle for tyre dealing.

53.   By 1926 houseboats were arriving in Church creek.

54.   Upson's hut was turned into tea rooms by Mrs. Fisher and her daughter Kath, seen here in 1928.

55. Mrs. Fisher feeds the ducks. Despite the bridge there was still access by water to the creek in 1928.

56. Benfleet Auction Rooms, seen in the background of 42, were busy in 1929. The building was demolished in 1961 to make way for the underpass road beneath the station.

57.   In 1900 the buildings of the timber wharf next to the *Hoy and Helmet* were thatched. The house on the left has now been demolished.

58. The tranquillity of old Benfleet is captured in this picture of Lower High Street and the *Hoy and Helmet*, taken in 1900.

59. Several of the buildings remain in 1991, but crossing the road is a little more hazardous.

60.   This 1916 postcard shows the hardway and the timber wharf adjoining the *Hoy and Helmet*. This is the wharf mentioned in the introduction for which a charge of £20 was made in 1559.

61.   Travel was by horse, not car, in 1925. There was much controversy in 1932 when planners sought to remove the *Crown* stables (in the centre), for road improvements. Between the stables and the inn, pedestrians took a short cut through an arch known as 'the hole in the wall'.

62.   In the High Street, around 1910 judging from the lad's clothes. Mr. Greig was a well-known host at the *Hoy and Helmet* for many years. Note the absence of the War Memorial.

63.   The same view, in 1990.

64. Looking down the High Street, Gray's sweet shop advertises Fred Attwell, who had an ironmonger's shop next door. Bill Attwell was the butcher in the next shop. On the right, next to the open door of the smithy, we see the skittle club advertised.

65. The back of the *Hoy and Helmet* being extended. In the background the building on the right is the smithy, and the skittle alley is on the left.

66.   The blacksmith's in 1910, between the *Hoy and Helmet* and the steps to the church. In the 18th century the smithy was built by the parish to give work to orphans and the poor for whom they were responsible. The land was given by the church. The building was demolished in 1950, and was replaced by a car park for the *Hoy and Helmet*. At this time the smith was Cyril Osborne, third from left.

67.   Inside the smithy Harry Thorogood (right) is assisted by Fred Taylor. Harry went to France in the First World War to shoe horses, and in 1936 Fred worked on building Essex Way. Villagers today can still remember sparks flying and horses waiting to be shod. Harry took over the business in the late 1920s and this picture was taken *c.*1925.

68. Charlie Tingey, with his wife Lily in 1925. Charlie took part in the National Shooting Championships at Bisley, and Benfleet Rifle Club still exists today. It was not unusual to find gunshops in villages at this time, as guns were used for poaching as well as sport.

69. Tuffield's store, on the left side of the High Street, opened in 1879. The same family owned it until 1934, when it was taken over by the Sugg family.

70. The same view in 1991.

71. Shops backing on to the church, in 1964. Lucy Marshall had the top shop for a florist while Grace and Dorothy Anderson kept the hairdresser's from 1930-45.

72. Knightley's shop, adjoining the main entrance to the church. The village institute, in which villagers were shareholders, is next door. It was in use as a public hall and Sunday School from 1892 to 1932.

73. In 1932 Knightley's shop and the village institute were demolished for road improvement. Note, on the corner of the Anchor, the sign 'Endway', now Essex Way.

74. A group in 1902 outside the *Anchor*. The lad on the left is Reg Tuffield, standing next to Mr. Boreham. The man in the centre with the beard is George Land, who had the inn from 1875, and he is holding his grand-daughter Dora Brand (later Hall). To her right is Mr. Francis and on the extreme right is Edie Nicholls.

75. Charlie Brand opened this shop at the *Anchor* in 1910. By 1913 the shop had closed and Laura, his wife, let the premises as a Post Office to the Lawrence family.

76. In 1905 a horse and carriage service from the *Anchor* was the only public transport.

77. By 1928 a bus service had begun. Driver and conductor are waiting to get on their bus to Southend. The service is still No. 3 today.

78. The first car in Benfleet was this Peugeot, in 1907. May Land is in the white blouse, and the driver is Mr. Jones, from Hadleigh woodyard. Four from the left is Kiff Layzell, 12 from left is Dick Alderton, on the extreme right is Fred Knightley, while three from the right is Mr. Francis. The lad is Fred Killingback.

79.   In 1915 Benfleet was asked to look after Belgian refugees, some of whom are pictured here, gathered round the Rev. Arthur Holthouse (centre of first seated row).

80.   The voluntary fire brigade acquired this engine in 1925. This is at the back of the *Anchor* and in the background is Teddy Land's wheelchair.

81. The fire brigade's garage was acquired in 1928, and moved to the side of the *Anchor* where there is now an electricity sub-station.

82. Ted Land was the fire brigade's first driver. At his wedding in 1934 to Mabel, 24 of his colleagues attended in their uniform and brass helmets, which were worn with pride.

83. Even when the new ambulance arrived the fire brigade was there to provide a guard of honour. *c.*1928.

84. This picture taken in 1900 shows George Land at the *Anchor* stables accompanied by his coachman, Teena Emberson. He took over the inn on 26 January 1875 and next day his books show that he paid £1 16s. for two gallons of Irish Whisky, £1 12s. for two gallons of rum, and £8 8s. for four barrels of beer.

85. Teddy Land's lamb was a familiar sight at the *Anchor*.

"I KNOW AN INN."

I know an Inn where they'll take you in,
If you only like to try;
So call at the 'Anchor' at Benfleet-on-Mud,
When you're feeling extra dry.
Teddy Land is the landlord, a jolly old sport,
You will always find him there;
He'll serve you in, and he'll serve you out,
But he always cheats you fair.

Chorus—

So here's good luck to the home-brewed stuff,
  And good luck to the thick and thin.
You can get what you want,
If you don't want tick,
  At the Benfleet 'Anchor' Inn.

The whisky's good and the beer not bad,
But the square-face is the best;
There's good entertainment for man and beast
At this ancient smuggler's rest.
You may play at crib, if you want a game,
And have plenty of time to spare,
But watch Old Ted when he shifts the pegs,
And see that he's marking square.

Chorus—

You'll hear such yarns in the private room
That you'll open wide your eyes;
They will tell you tales of the Buster days.
And a pack of blooming lies.
They will talk of the time of the Canvey plots,
When good lunches to all were free;
Of Amsterdam and of Rotterdam,
And of many a damn good spree.

S. SODDY, *Italy, Nov. 28, 1918.*

86. Such was the fame of the *Anchor* that this song was printed in India in 1918.

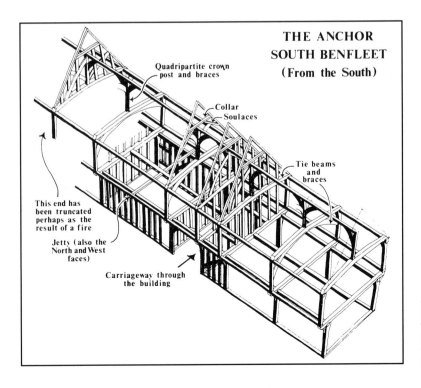

**THE ANCHOR
SOUTH BENFLEET
(From the South)**

Quadripartite crown post and braces

Collar
Soulaces

Tie beams
and
braces

This end has
been truncated
perhaps as the
result of a fire

Jetty (also the
North and West
faces)

Carriageway through
the building

87. This sketch was produced by the Planning Department of Essex County Council after the finds of 1989. It shows the timber frame of *c.*1381 which originally extended into the road, towards the church.

Barstable Hundred

Parishes	Persons Licenced	Signs	Sureties
Benfleet North	Sharpe Thomas	Harrow	Thos. Newland, Henry Jenkings,
Benfleet South	Brewitt Ann	Blue Anchor	Phillip Tabor, Joseph Amiss,
	Foster Stephen	Hoy	Phillip Tabor, Joseph Amiss,
	Greenaway Haggar	World's End	James White, Phillip Head,
	Spanner William	Chequer	Thos. Newland, Henry Jenkins,
	Watson William	Crown	Mathew Took, Stephen Foster,

88. This entry in the 1770 Register of Ale-houses shows the original name, *Blue Anchor.*

89. The roof beams in the bar
which helped date the *Anchor.*

90. The impressive and original crown posts in the roof.

91. Armorial bearings found on the first floor tie beams, with original decoration to the right.

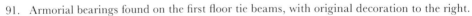

92 a & b.   Medieval windows were
uncovered on the first floor. These are in
the present back wall facing the stables,
and between the existing windows.

93.   The War Memorial was dedicated on 30 May 1920. The administration of the allotments on the right, now a public car park, brought about the formation of the present Benfleet Horticultural Society.

94.   Five elms grew outside Anchor Cottages in 1920, just before the memorial was erected.

95.   Removal of the elm trees reveals the cottage in which Lizzie Thurlow lived. She was a merry soul who went round singing hymns and, on returning from the *Anchor* on Saturday nights, would lie with her feet out of the top window. A horse trough (removed in 1932 for road improvements to Cemetery Corner) was installed opposite the *Anchor* to mark the coronation of King George V in 1911. On the first night it was in place, Lizzie used it for her washing.

96.   This little girl, photographed in 1912, leaves behind two horses about to move a large stack of hay and walks across the original village green, now a public car park.

97. The *Anchor* meadows, now an electricity substation, were the venue for the annual fête, seen here in 1908.

98. The two buildings of the Benfleet National School, built in School Lane in 1845 and used until 1931. Robert Hall was headmaster from 1893 to 1923 and this picture was presented to him on his last day, 28 March 1923. This area is now a large public car park.

99. From School Lane, through the Downs, to the ferry. This ancient road was probably used by the Danes in 893 and was the only way to Canvey until 1850. This picture was taken in 1925 and the path still exists today.

100.   The corner of School Lane, looking up Essex Way, in 1925. The Methodist church was built here in 1877. Suttons Farm is in the background. This site is now a factory and doctor's surgery.

101.   Further up Essex Way (then East Street and later Endway) was Sleepy Hollow Cottage seen here in 1910.

102. Cottages in Essex Way at the corner of Grosvenor Road, in 1908.

103. This shows most of the cottages pictured above in 1961, and about to be demolished. They were originally poor houses owned by the parish, who sold them in 1843.

104. In 1991 one cottage, The Moorings, remains.

105. Essex Way, in 1925. This looks towards the memorial: Norwood Drive would be on the right at the five-bar gate in the distance. It was this gate which signified the end of the old East Street, hence Endway. Sam Wilkins, the vet, had his premises by the gate. Many of these properties remain today.

106. Browne's Cottages in 1925. This joins the previous photograph.

107. The footpath shown here in 1919 leads to the gate and Browne's Cottages (shown in 106). Essex Way follows the same route.

108.   Essex Way was opened in 1937.

109. This picture of the parish church of St Mary the Virgin in 1909 shows the timber porch, erected late in the 15th century and considered to be one of the most beautiful in the country.

110. This side of the church, also photographed in 1909, shows the now bricked-up northern entrance used by the bailiff. The children are, left to right, Edna Quilter, Ruby Ross, Olive Ross and Digby Young.

111. Inside the church in 1912. Note the position of the organ, which is now at the back of the church. The chancel screen, added in 1929 has paintings by Miss Barbara Nicholson of six male and six female saints. As a model for St Christopher she used the ferryman, Ted Edwards.

112. There are six bells in the tower, one from the 15th century, while the others were made in 1636, 1664, 1676, 1790 and 1949. The latest bell, the treble, was added as a thanksgiving for victory in the war and this picture shows the Rev. Leighton Houghton with the bells about to be re-hung, in 1949.

113. A view towards Vicarage Hill in 1912. The white cattle rail gave protection to pedestrians. The road was often flooded by the stream to Church creek in the dip by the cottages. In 1926 the road was raised and today only the top of the *Anchor* wall can be seen.

114. Church Cottages. Note the rails on the right over the stream which used to go along the back of the *Anchor*.

115. Church Cottages in 1910. In the background, between the trees, there is a rare view of Hall Farm buildings. The farm's historic thatched barn, 400 years old, can be seen at the roadside.

116. The view towards the church in 1913.

117. By 1955 the thatched barn has become tin-roofed. Hall Farm Cottages were demolished soon after this.

118. The bottom of Vicarage Hill in 1921. In the distance, on the left, is Sweet Briar Cottage, part of the farm of that name and now replaced by the police station.

119. Sweet Briar Cottage on the left, looking towards the War Memorial.

120. The Rev. Charles Box walks up Vicarage Hill, to the vicarage, in 1910. This was the road to Southend up to 1937: the author recalls in that year cycling from school in Southend, home to Canvey, and, on reaching the bottom of this hill, failing to stop and finishing in the fields adjoining the Methodist church.

121. The formality of a 1907 vicarage garden party is captured in this picture.

122. The High Road between Green Road and Hope Road in 1933. The first building on the left, with the ornate roofwork, is Barnes' shop.

123 a & b.   Land for the Methodist church was acquired in 1927 at the bottom of Vicarage Hill. The opening ceremony took place on 8 April 1931 and the poster advertising it is illustrated.

124.   Liberty Market Stores in the High Road, now Barnes', was run by Mr. Wheeley, when biscuits were 6d. a pound and a quarter of tea was 6½d.

125. The junction of High Road with Brook Road. This was the position of Hopes Green hence the name of the stores. The building on the right was a cinema.

126. The same view today. Many of the buildings still remain above the later 20th-century shopfronts.

127. Moving down the High Road, westwards, the building on the right was the original Hopes Green Post Office. Today it is Belgravia Florist.

128.   Benfleet Hall was built in Brook Road in 1922. It is now a clothing factory.

129 a & b.   In the High Road, opposite Brook Road, Jack Searson is standing outside his shoe shop on the day it closed in 1989. The other picture shows the shop opening in 1926. Jack is standing next to his father. Note that they moved from their original shop to a new one they had built next door in 1959.

130.   The picture is marked 1927, so the school (on the right) in London Road had only recently been opened. The baker's, woodyard and pumping station exist today, but the house on the left, 'The Limes', does not.

131.   The Parade was built in 1928 by Raffin and Bonser. The initials and date above the shops are visible today. Although the shop fronts have changed, most remain as built. This shows the south side.

132. The north side has changed even less. In the distance is 'The Limes'.

133. The Parade in 1952 is little different from today.

134. Outside the cottage visible above the van in the previous picture there was a board with letters screwed to it proudly proclaiming 'T. Dean – Chimney Sweep'.

135. Having left Cemetery Corner the carriage, in 1912, is approaching the site of the Parade. The site of the *Appleton Arms* is on the immediate right and 'The Limes' stands out.

136. Looking down High Road from Cemetery Corner in 1915. Doris Knightley is on her father's bicycle.

137. The High Road at Cemetery Corner in 1929, looking north to Tarpots. The new burial ground was built by the District Council in 1912 for about £300, and gave the corner its name.

138.   Tarpots Corner from the south.

139.   The two vehicles have just left Tarpots heading for Cemetery Corner. The *Tarpot* public house was built behind the man and his dog. This postcard dates from *c*.1911.

140. Tarpots Farm in 1905 is destined to become Shafer's Shopping Arcade.

141.   Thundersley Park Road in 1921. The house on the right has become Stafford Hall Rest Home and the other houses also still exist.

142.   The same view today. It is interesting to see how, once again, the road follows the line of the old footpath.

143.   Thundersley Park Road at the junction with Avondale Road in 1928.

144.   Hope Road, 1926.

145. In 1946 Hope Road had a Victory street party. Arthur Cox, Methodist Sunday School Superintendent, is on the left.

146. Houses in Church Road, now Hall Farm Road, in 1913. The houses, backing on the railway, were built in 1902 and remain today.

147. The Mothers' Union outside St Mary's church hall in School Lane in 1951. Top row, from left: Elsie Dryden, Alice Sidebotham, Mrs. Mildenhall, ?, Eileen Lawrence, Helen Cole, Lucy Marshall, ?, ?, Mrs. Wilder, Lassie Brown, Doris Schooling, Mrs. Matson, Mrs. Watts, Mary Murray, Laura Brand and Mrs. Marchant, the Rev. Reuben Henthorne (centre); bottom row from left: ?, Doris Hawtin, Frances Austen, Lucy Barnard and Mrs. Pearcey.

148. A concert party in Benfleet Hall.

149. Although the new junior school opened in High Road in 1927 this shows a class at the School Lane building in 1931. Gilbert Wines on left, elbows on table, five from the right; second row (arms folded), Vera Quilter (author's wife); and front row, five from left, Barbara Stacey.

150. The ladies of 1909, possibly the Mother's Union with the Rev. Charles Box.

151. 1906 school group, with Mr. Hall. Front row standing, third from right, Edna Brand; behind her to the left, Ruby Ross; and next to her to the right, Olive Ross.

152.   In 1925 South Benfleet Cricket Club played at a ground behind houses in Fleet Road. Standing, from left to right: Harry Phillips (*Hoy*), W. Harmer, L. Hill, Stan Fisher, K. McWilton, W. Newton, (umpire?);seated: T. Barber, S. Harvey, H. Pauldon, R. McWilton and G. Bremner; front row: L. Arnop and S. Harmer.

153.   Did they put as much effort into the cricket as they clearly did into the fancy dress? This photograph was taken in 1910.

154. The Benfleet Football Club in 1922. Top right: trainer, Mr. Cook (the postman); third from right, Albert Gladwin; extreme left, Fred Knightley; centre: right Guy Revell, bottom, centre, Ernie Quilter.

⚜ Admit Bearer ⚜

TO THE

SOUTH BENFLEET
Grand Jubilee Celebration Fete,
— With TEA, —
TO BE HELD
in the MEADOW, adjoining SUTTON'S FARM,
ON WEDNESDAY, JUNE 23rd, 1897.
COMMENCING AT 2 P.M.

No. 5

T. ALAN READ, Hon. Sec.

1837 – 1897

Presented by Mrs. G. H. Ross.

155. The ticket issued to Emily Nicholls for the 1897 Jubilee Fête at Suttons Farm in Essex Way.

156. In 1917 these four bombs were dropped by a Zeppelin on Mr. Bingham's garden at the corner of Hope Road and High Road.

157. The vicarage grounds were the venue for many annual events and fêtes. The scouts, under Skipper Fisher, used the vicarage garage until the Second World War.

No. 1910

SOUTH BENFLEET SCOUT COMMITTEE.

Admit Bearer to .

FETE,

In aid of the ESSEX PRISONERS OF WAR,

TO BE HELD IN THE

Vicarage Grounds, South Benfleet,

—ON—

Monday, August 5th, 1918, commencing 2.30 p.m.

Tickets—6d. each.   Children under 14—3d.

CONVENIENT *Semi-detached* BUNGALOW

PRICE £325 (Cash £315) FREEHOLD

LIVING ROOM   Fitted with modern tiled open grate with oak mantel.
Electric plug.

Gas fire in Front Bedroom.

KITCHENETTE   Enamelled copper deep sink and draining board, tiled floor

BATHROOM   Fitted with porcelain enamel bath with gas geyser over.

REPAYMENTS   £1-13-9 per month   Equivalent to 7/9 weekly

RATES (including Water)   —   —   3/6 per week

158. The opening of Benfleet Downs on 14 July 1934 by Sir Edgar Bonham Carter, K.C.M.G., Vice Chairman of the Open Spaces Preservation Society (centre right). Also present are Councillor T. J. Evans, chairman of the Benfleet Urban District Council (wearing his chain of office), Councillor Walter Johnson, Chairman and Councillor L. J. Rivett, Vice-Chairman of the Open Spaces Committee, the Rev. Ralph Gardner, Vicar of South Benfleet (third to right of Council Chairman) and the original land owner Frank Barnes.

159. This was some of the sales literature produced when the Southdown Estate was built at Cemetery Corner in 1936.

160. This aerial view of Benfleet in 1948 shows, in the top left corner, the army camp which was built in the Recreation Ground during the war. It was roughly on the site of the estate in which the roads are named after birds. The trees to the left of the camp are at the east end of Woodham Road, and are reaching towards the bottom of Appleton Road. Houses to the right of the camp are in Brook Road.

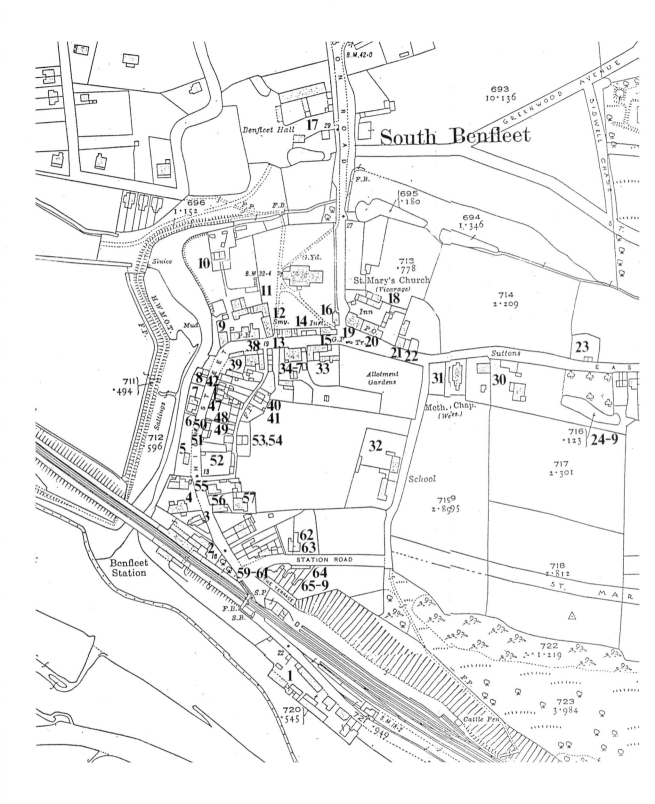

161. Ordnance Survey map issued 1922. The horse trough erected in 1911 opposite the *Anchor* is shown but the War Memorial is not. The position of Benfleet Hall and Hall Farm is shown at the top (no.17). The list shows residents in the 1925-30 period but some changes took place.

1. Leigh Building Supply Wharf
2. Station-Master Dollard/Knight
3. O. I. C. Powell
4. Ross/Lamb
5. Auction rooms/granary
6. Killingback
7. Revell
8. Gladwin
9. Phillips/Greig (*Hoy*)
10. Young
11. Skittle alley
12. Osborne/Thorogood, blacksmith
13. Wright
14. Tingay/Anderson
15. The Institute
16. Knightley
17. The Hall, Hall Farm
18. Tom Land
19. Ted Land (*Anchor*)
20. Lawrence (Post Office)
21. Dulake
22. Hockley
23. Williamson
24. Rowe
25. Williams
26. St Ledger
27. Thorogood
28. Richardson
29. Clubb
30. Barnes (Suttons Farm)
31. Methodist church
32. National School
33. Tuffield (grocer)
34. Attwell (hardware)
35. Attwell (butcher)
36. Lumley (cakes)
37. Low (fish)
38. Gray (sweets)
39. Simmons (*Crown*)
40. Cripps
41. Stacey
42. Revell
43. Layzell
44. Jennings
45. Argent
46. Mee
47. Hands
48. Valentine
49. Joe Brown
50. Marie Welsh (hairdresser)
51. Bishop (clockmaker)
52. Sheppard (shoes)
53. Yeldham
54. Lamley
55. Mitchell (store)
56. Duttons/Shiner and Holmes (drapers)
57. The Manor House
58. Francis
59. Pease
60. Wines
61. Marchant (shop)
62. Parker
63. Howard (school)
64. Slaughter house
65. Hart (butcher)
66. Hunt
67. Ellard
68. Ellard
69. Claxton

162.   This view of Benfleet, taken by Edward Clack in 1990, shows the old village with modern development beyond. The *Anchor* buildings dominate the village and the way in which the end of the inn (nearer the church) has been truncated can be seen.